Awesome Animal Skills

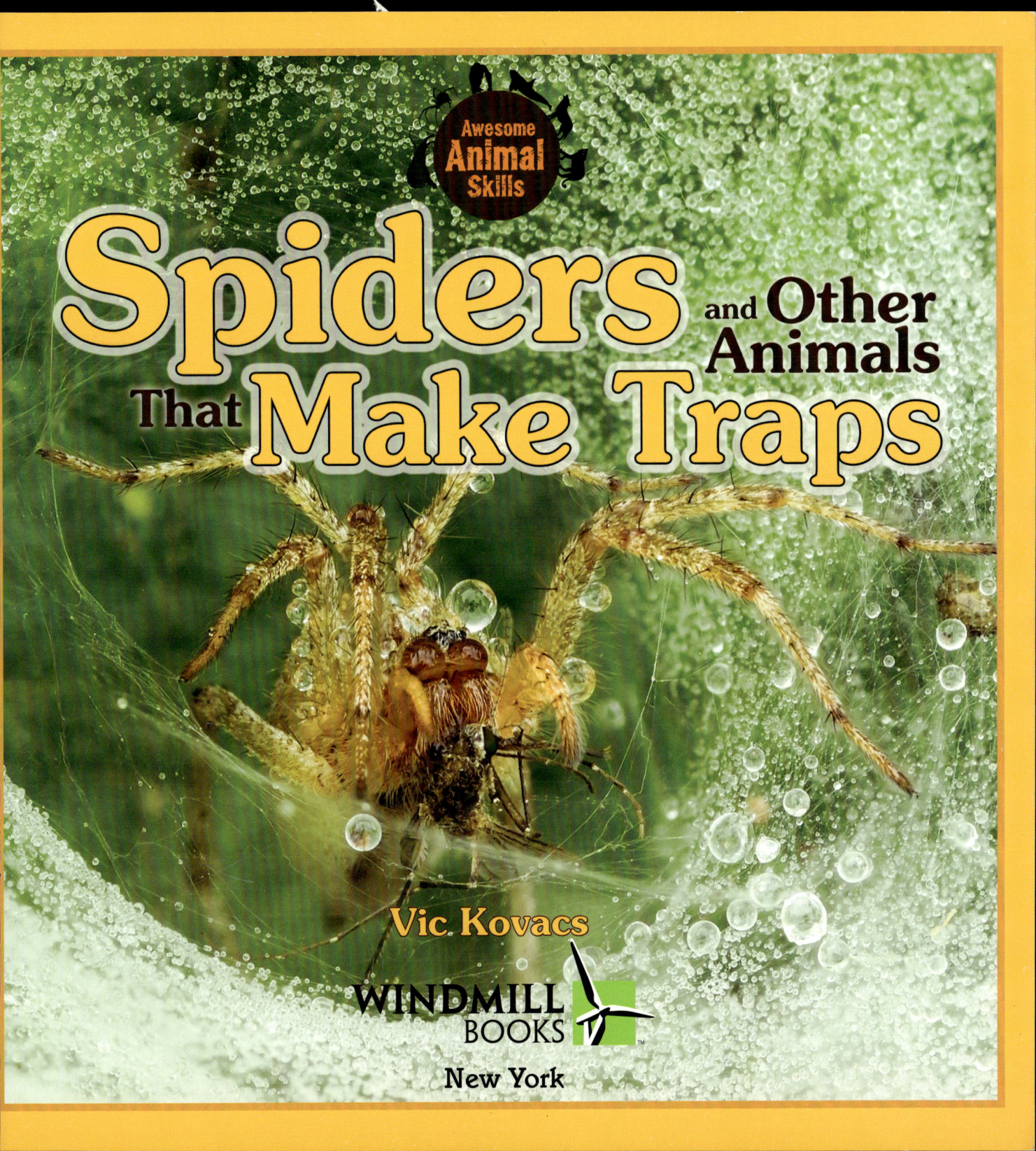

Spiders and Other Animals That Make Traps

Vic Kovacs

WINDMILL BOOKS
New York

Published in 2016 by **Windmill Books**,
an Imprint of Rosen Publishing
29 East 21st Street, New York, NY 10010

Copyright © 2016 by The Rosen Publishing Group, Inc.

All rights reserved. No part of this book may be reproduced in any form
without permission in writing from the publisher, except by a reviewer.

Developed and produced for Rosen by BlueAppleWorks Inc.

Art Director: T.J. Choleva
Managing Editor for BlueAppleWorks: Melissa McClellan
Designer: Joshua Avramson
Photo Research: Jane Reid
Editor: Marcia Abramson

Photo Credits:
Cover left, p. 7 Paul Looyen/Shutterstock; cover, p. 5 LorraineHudgins/Shutterstock; title page Anton Kozyrev/Shutterstock; back cover, TOC top Musat/Thinkstock; TOC bottom Ken Hoehn/Thinkstock; p. 4 top left LaDonna Brezik/Shutterstock; p. 4 top Balazs Justin/Shutterstock; p.4 Dmitrijs Bindemanis/Shutterstock; p 5 top iceink/Shutterstock; p. 6 top left Piyathep/Shutterstock; p. 6 top Boykung/Shutterstock; p. 6 left Mixrinho/Shutterstock; p. 6-7 EBFoto/Shutterstock; p. 8 top left Dr. Morley Read/Shutterstock; p. 8 top Aleksey Stemmer/Shutterstock; p. 8 Vincent de Groot/Creative Commons; p. 9 Toby Hudson/Creative Commons; p. 9 top Yathin S Krishnappa/Creative Commons; p. 10 top left, 10 right GalliasM/Creative Commons; p. 10 top, 10 left Ingi Agnarsson, Matjaž Kuntner, Todd A. Blackledge/Creative Commons; p. 10-11 Hugh Lansdown/Shutterstock; P. 11 Brberrys/Shutterstock; p. 11 right Peter Waters/Shutterstock; p. 12 top left Peter Waters/Shutterstock; p. 12 top Sarin Kunthong/Shutterstock; p. 12 Robyn Butler/Shutterstock; p. 13 top JonRichfield/Creative Commons; p. 13 Hmendoza356 Deisy Mendoza/Creative Commons; p. 14 top left, 15 top, 15 Fritz Geller-Grimm/Creative Commons; p. 14 top Joanna Zopoth-Lipiejko/Shutterstock; p. 14 left Akio Tanikawa/Creative Commons; p. 14-15 zstock/Shutterstock; p. 16 top left Markrosenrosen/Creative Commons; p. 16 top Pseudopanax/Public Domain; p. 16 Brian Brake/Science Photo Library; p. 17 Mnolf/Creative Commons; p. 18 top left Melinda Fawver/Shutterstock; p. 18 top Queserasera99/Thinkstock; P. 18 left TanerYILDIRIM/Thinkstock; p. 18 errnir/Shutterstock; p. 19 Alash/Creative Commons; p. 19 left, right Scott Robinson/Creative Commons; p. 20 top left Heiko Kiera/Shutterstock; p. 20 top Richard A McMillin/Shutterstock; p. 20-21 passion4nature/Thinkstock; p. 21Jupiterimages/Thinkstock; p. 22 top left, 23 Feng Yu/Shutterstock; p. 22 top Richard Fitzer/Shutterstock; p. 22-23 Tania Thomson/Shutterstock; p. 22 right Four Oaks/Shutterstock; p. 24 top left April Nobile/AntWeb.org/CC-BY-SA-3.0; p. 24 top Mr. Suttipon Yakham/Shutterstock; p 24-25 Matteis/Look At Sciences/Science Photo Library; p. 26 top left Eduard Kyslynskyy/Shutterstock; p. 26 top Stephan Morris/Shutterstock; p. 26 Robert L Kothenbeutel/Shutterstock; p. 27 left Mihail Zhukov/Thinkstock; p. 27 Arto Hakola/Shutterstock;p. 28 top leftjuk atrasat/Shutterstock; p. 28 top Decha Thapanya/Shutterstock; p. 28 Nathanael Siders/Shutterstock; p. 28-29 michael watson/Shutterstock; p. 29 Ra'id Khalil/Shutterstock.

Cataloging-in-Publication-Data
Kovacs, Vic.
Spiders and other animals that make traps / by Vic Kovacs.
p. cm. — (Awesome animal skills)
Includes index.
ISBN 978-1-4777-5655-3 (pbk.)
ISBN 978-1-4777-5654-6 (6 pack)
ISBN 978-1-4777-5586-0 (library binding)
1. Spiders — Juvenile literature. 2. Animal behavior — Juvenile literature.
3. Predatory animals — Juvenile literature. I. Title.
QL458.4 K68 2016
595.4'4—d23

Manufactured in the United States of America
CPSIA Compliance Information: Batch #WS15WM: For Further Information contact: Rosen Publishing, New York, New York at 1-800-237-9932

CONTENTS

Deadly Traps	4
Mysterious Spiders	6
Deadly Webs	8
Amazing Webs	10
Special-Skills Spiders	12
Hunting Without a Web	14
Tricky Glowworms	16
Ruthless Antlions	18
Shrewd Alligators	20
Burrowing Owls	22
Amazonian Ants	24
Mesmerizing Stoats	26
Assassin Bugs	28
Glossary	30
For More Information	31
Index	32

DEADLY TRAPS

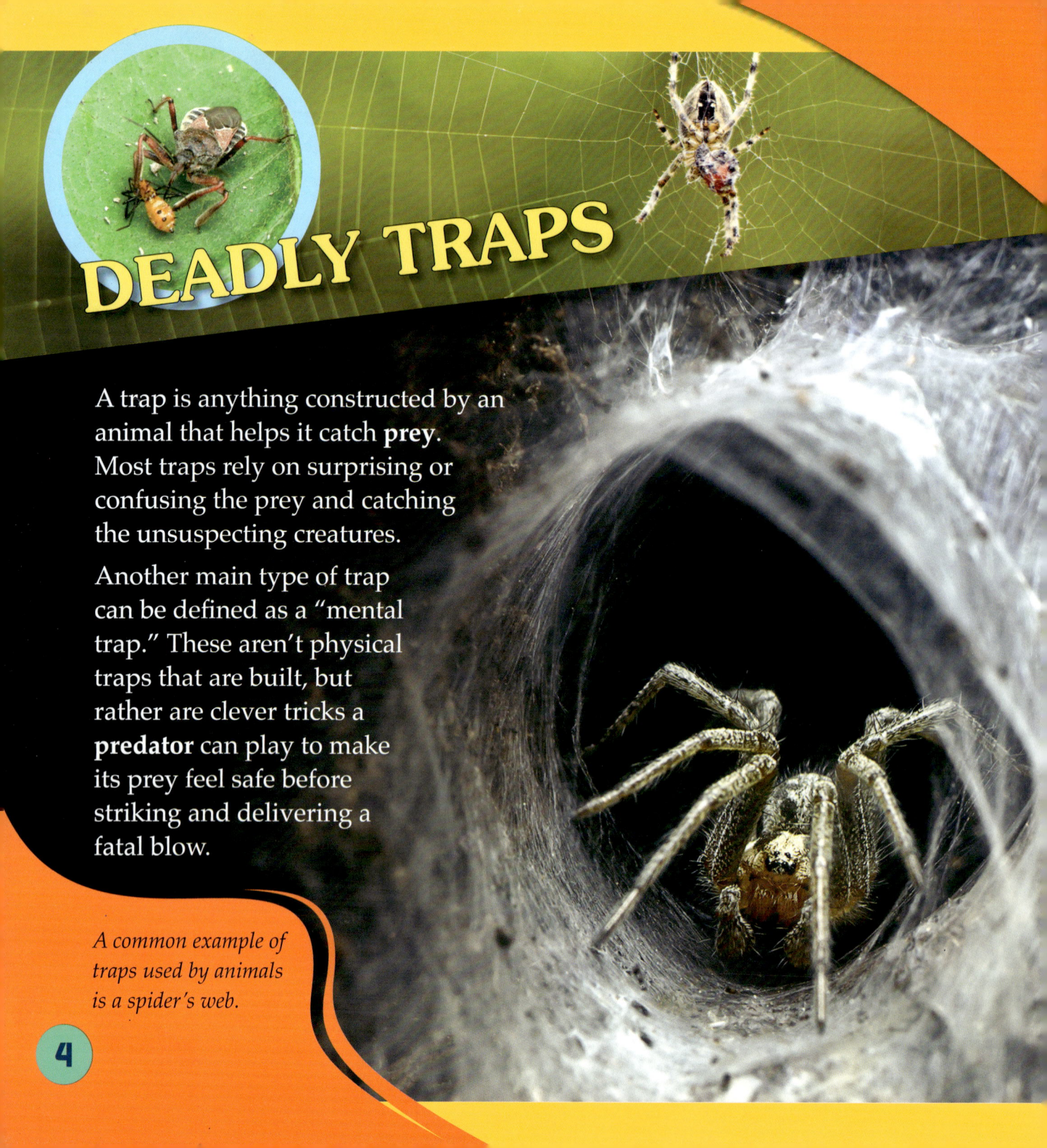

A trap is anything constructed by an animal that helps it catch **prey**. Most traps rely on surprising or confusing the prey and catching the unsuspecting creatures.

Another main type of trap can be defined as a "mental trap." These aren't physical traps that are built, but rather are clever tricks a **predator** can play to make its prey feel safe before striking and delivering a fatal blow.

A common example of traps used by animals is a spider's web.

WHY USE TRAPS?

For predators, there are many benefits to using traps. Animals are able to save energy by not going after their prey, but simply waiting for prey to fall in a trap. Trap-using animals often need less food to survive than predators who use more common methods of hunting.

Probably the best part about this hunting method is that it greatly reduces the danger to the attacker. Confused or entangled prey usually can no longer strike back.

*Antlion **larvae** dig sandpit traps to catch ants. They use their abdomen as a plow to shovel the soil.*

When it comes to spiders, using traps has the added benefit of allowing the predator to devour its prey whenever it wants.

MYSTERIOUS SPIDERS

Spiders usually have eight eyes. Some have fewer. Most cannot see very well with them.

SPIDERS EVERYWHERE

Spiders are not insects, as many people believe. They're actually arachnids. The main difference is that insects only have six legs, and spiders (and all other arachnids) have eight. The biggest difference between spiders and other animals is the spinneret. These organs, located in the tip of the abdomen, are what allow spiders to weave the silk that they make their famous webs with. Once prey are caught in webs, spiders use their other biggest weapon, their jaws. Spider jaws are equipped with fangs that inject prey with **venom** that either kills or otherwise knocks the prey out. Spiders exist in virtually every environment on earth. In fact, no matter where you are, be it a forest, a beach, or even your own house, you're probably only a few feet from a spider!

DID YOU KNOW?

It is estimated that one acre (0.4 ha) of meadowland can support over two million spiders.

The vast majority of spiders hunt and live alone. There are some social species, but they are largely outnumbered.

DEADLY WEBS

The most well-known type of spider web is the orb web. Everyone has seen one of these wheel-shaped webs. They are often hung between the branches of a tree, or blades of grass in a garden. Their clever design covers a large area while using the least possible amount of spider silk.

Orb weavers only make up about 10 percent of known spider species. Other types of web include funnel webs, in which spiders hide until an insect wanders across a **protruding** sheet of webs. There are also **scaffold**, or tangle webs. Those are generally built flat horizontally, just a little ways off the ground.

THREADS OF A WEB

Spiders have a lot of amazing abilities. The fact that they build their webs from a substance produced by their own bodies might be the most amazing of all. A common orb web is made with at least four different types of thread, all from the same spider. These different types of silk, and their different uses, have allowed spiders to adapt to almost every environment without having to actually **evolve** into different body types as many other animals did.

Spider web threads transmit vibrations telling a spider that it has caught its prey. Social species use these vibrations to communicate with each other.

Funnel web spiders live in moist and sheltered **habitats**, such as under rocks and in and under rotting logs.

AMAZING WEBS

Darwin's bark spider was discovered in Madagascar in 2009. The spiders are named for scientist Charles Darwin and for their appearance. They are small, about one inch (2.5 cm), and some have **camouflage** that makes them look like tree bark or leaf. It's easy to see why they were not noticed for so long. With their camouflage and small size (one inch), it's understandable that they went unnoticed for so long. But what definitely should not have escaped notice are their giant webs. Darwin's bark spider likes to build its web across bodies of water. Starting on one side of a river, they'll release a strand of silk into the wind. When it catches onto something on the other side, they get to work. Some webs grow to 30 square feet (2.8 sq m), making them the world's largest.

Females sometimes kill and eat the males after mating. This unusual behavior gave the widow its name.

DID YOU KNOW?

Darwin's bark spider doesn't just weave one of the largest known webs, it also weaves the strongest. The silk that makes up its web has been described as the toughest biological substance ever studied. It's ten times as strong as Kevlar, the material used to make bulletproof vests.

DEADLY WIDOW

Black widows are one of the most widely known and feared spiders in the world because of their strong venom. However, what is truly special about the black widow is its web. Called a scaffold, sheet, or tangle web, these are generally built flat horizontally, just a little ways off the ground. The webs often look like a tangled mess, hence their name. In reality, they are often very carefully designed. The widow will hang underneath the sheet until an insect bumps into the top of it. Once the prey gets stuck, the widow runs over and bites it. The prey dies from the powerful venom that the bite injects.

SPECIAL-SKILLS SPIDERS

The net-throwing, or ogre-faced, spider has a special way to catch prey. First, it weaves a scaffold to work on. On this surface it weaves a rectangular web. It grasps the four corners of the rectangle with its four front legs. It then cuts the rectangle off the scaffold, causing the stretchy, net-like web to contract to much smaller than its original size. At this point, depending on whether the spider eats flying or crawling insects, it will stay aloft in its scaffold or crawl down to just above the ground. When an insect flies or crawls by, the spider then stretches the net open and ensnares its prey, or in some cases, drops the net onto the prey from above.

Ogre-faced spiders have six eyes. Two larger ones give night vision for hunting.

WEB WRITING

The yellow garden spider is also known as the writing spider. This is because it decorates its orb web with extra silk that looks like writing. The "writing" has a unique zigzag pattern. It can appear as a single line near the middle of the web, or up to four lines making an X in the web's center. One theory says that spiders use the zigzag pattern for camouflage, hiding behind it so that insects are unaware they're there. Another theory says that spiders decorate their webs to make them more visible, so that larger animals like birds won't fly into them, destroying the spider's hard work.

Decorative silk is also called a stabilimentum.

HUNTING WITHOUT A WEB

For some spiders, weaving silk is a fairly minor, if not completely unnecessary part of the hunt. The trapdoor spider, for instance, digs a **burrow** in the ground. On top of this hole, it weaves a trapdoor that it uses to hide itself. Some species set up a system of silk tripwires leading to the burrow entrance, so they can tell when prey is approaching from farther away. Other simpler species simply lie in wait under their trapdoor, relying on vibrations sent through the ground to tell when their next meal is on its way past. Trapdoor spiders are also known for being incredibly fast, being able to strike their prey in only 0.03 seconds.

A hinged trapdoor is made of silk, dirt, and plant matter. It is hard to see even in daylight.

14

SPITTING SPIDERS

Finally, we come to the most unique way spiders trap their prey: spitting. The Scytodidae family of spiders have developed specialized venom glands that produce an incredible liquid that hardens on contact. The spider shoots two streams of this substance at its prey, one from either fang. This not only stops the prey from being able to move, but also attaches it to whatever surface it is on. The spider is then free to wrap and ingest its prey whenever it desires.

Like other spiders, the spitting spider injects venom into captured prey and wraps it in silk.

Spitting spiders sway rapidly side-to-side when attacking, so the silk forms a zigzag pattern. An attack takes just a fraction of a second.

TRICKY GLOWWORMS

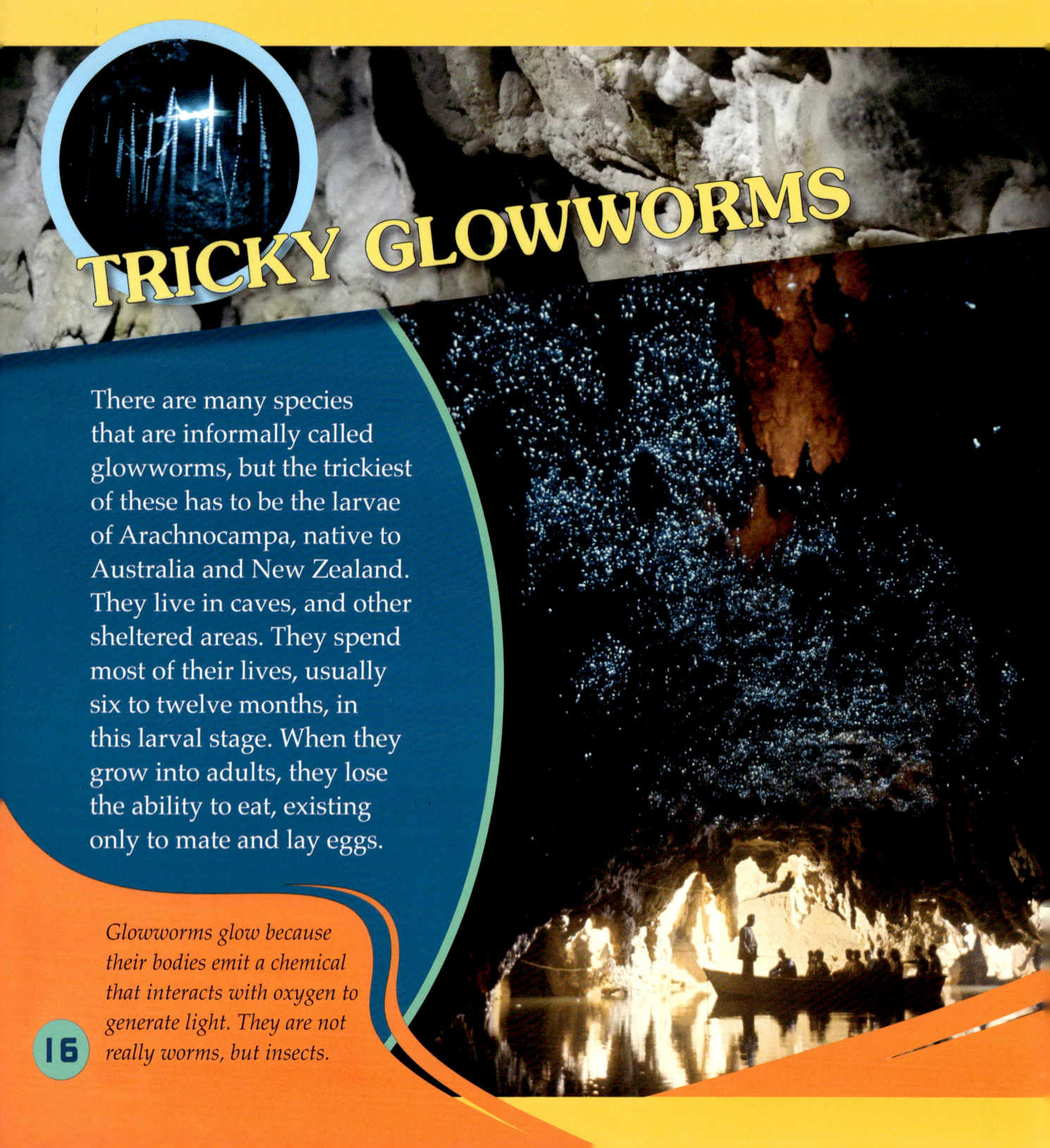

There are many species that are informally called glowworms, but the trickiest of these has to be the larvae of Arachnocampa, native to Australia and New Zealand. They live in caves, and other sheltered areas. They spend most of their lives, usually six to twelve months, in this larval stage. When they grow into adults, they lose the ability to eat, existing only to mate and lay eggs.

Glowworms glow because their bodies emit a chemical that interacts with oxygen to generate light. They are not really worms, but insects.

DID YOU KNOW?

A hungry glowworm will glow much more brightly than one that has just eaten.

The chemical that makes glowworms glow so brightly also makes them taste bad. This helps to keep predators away.

ALLURING LIGHTS

Much like a spider, the glowworm also uses threads of silk to catch prey, but in a much different way. The glowworm spins itself a silk nest on the ceiling of its cave and then hangs down up to 70 individual threads all around it. Then, to attract its prey, it starts to glow. A full ceiling of glowworms actually resembles a night sky filled with stars, which might be why prey is attracted to them. The prey think they're moving outside, toward the sky. They're actually flying directly into the glowworm's sticky strands of silk, which the glowworm immediately hoists up to begin enjoying its meal.

RUTHLESS ANTLIONS

Named after their love of devouring their favorite prey, antlions are actually the larval form of an insect that resembles a dragonfly when fully grown. Commonly found in deserts and other sandy areas, they have a seed-shaped body with huge, toothy jaws. These needle-like teeth can pierce its victim's body and suck out its fluids. In some species, these teeth can also inject venom, which liquefies the prey's innards, much like a spider.

SLIPPERY SANDS

Antlions make their traps by walking in backwards circles in the sand, digging a burrow with their legs and tossing additional sand out with their jaws. When they're done, the burrow is about 1 to 1.5 inches (2.5 to 3.8 cm) across, and about that deep. They then hide at the bottom, with nothing but their massive jaws visible, waiting for an ant or other insect to blunder by. The prey will immediately begin to slip into the hole, and the loose sand that makes up the walls prevent any hope of escape. Just to be sure, the antlion will often toss up additional sand, creating landslides. The prey is then grabbed by the antlion's powerful jaws and sucked dry. The prey's husk is then tossed out of the burrow, and the antlion waits for its next victim.

DID YOU KNOW?

Antlions are called "doodlebugs" because of the long, wandering trails they leave in sand while trying to find suitable spots to dig their burrows.

An antlion hides on the bottom of its trap with only its jaws showing.

SHREWD ALLIGATORS

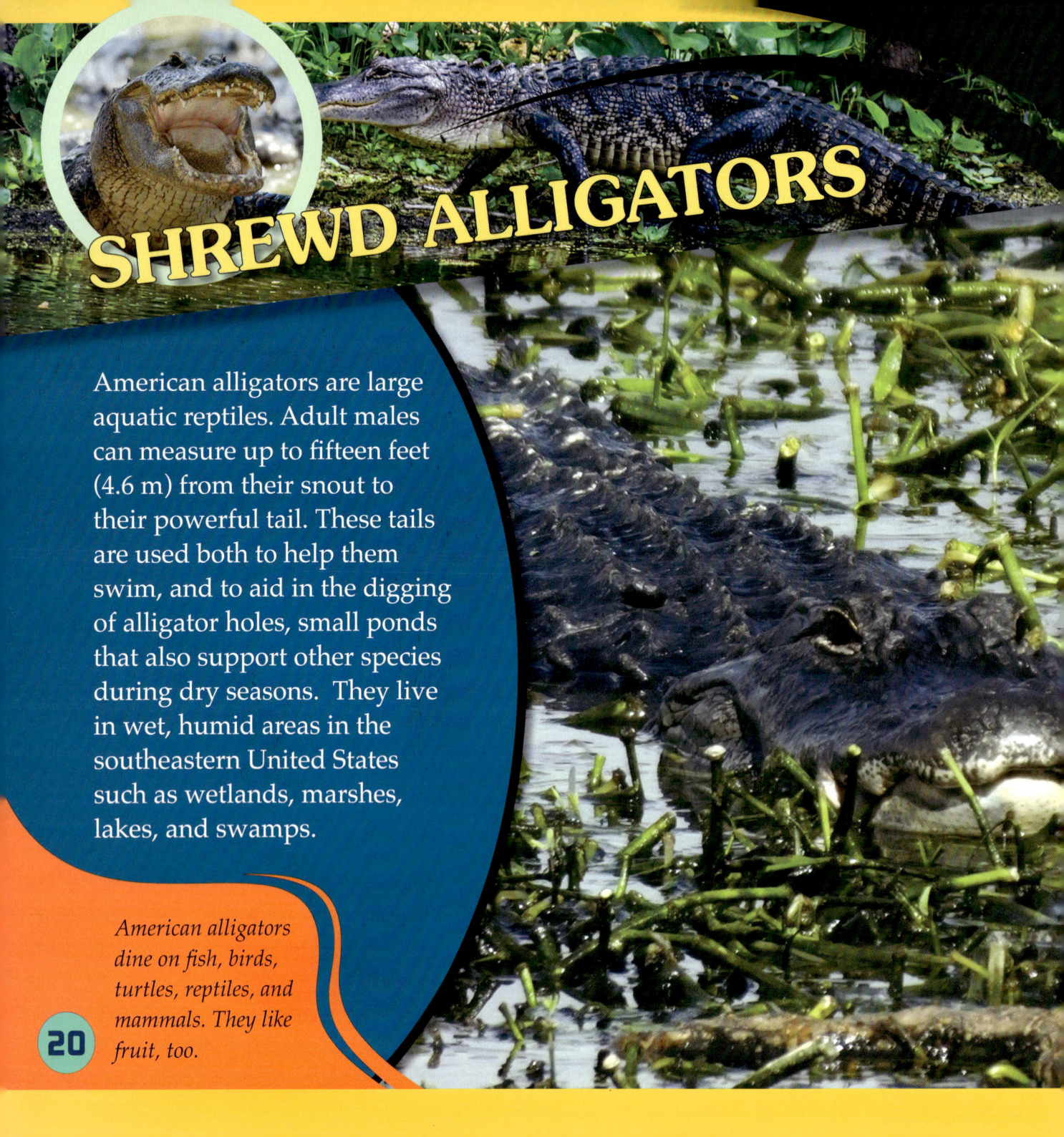

American alligators are large aquatic reptiles. Adult males can measure up to fifteen feet (4.6 m) from their snout to their powerful tail. These tails are used both to help them swim, and to aid in the digging of alligator holes, small ponds that also support other species during dry seasons. They live in wet, humid areas in the southeastern United States such as wetlands, marshes, lakes, and swamps.

American alligators dine on fish, birds, turtles, reptiles, and mammals. They like fruit, too.

BRAINS AND BRAWN

American alligators are considered apex predators, which means they're at the apex, or top of the food chain in their habitats. They use a variety of hunting methods to capture all kinds of prey, from insects and snails as hatchlings, to fish and mammals as adults. Its most clever method for securing food is how it tricks birds during their nesting season. The alligator will balance sticks and twigs on its snout, not moving a muscle for hours. When a bird stops by, it thinks it has found some materials to help it build a nest. When it approaches the alligator, the predator makes its move, lunging at the bird and crushing it with its powerful jaws.

Five million American alligators live in the southeast United States, especially Florida.

DID YOU KNOW?

This behavior is the first time a reptile has been seen to use tools. It's also the first time a predator has been known to time its use of lures to seasonal behavior of other animals, in this case, birds' nesting periods.

BURROWING OWLS

Burrowing owls are fairly small, about 6 to 12 inches (15 to 30 cm) tall, with a wingspan of up to two feet (61 cm). They live all over North and South America. They make their nests underground in burrows, often built and abandoned by other animals, such as prairie dogs.

Burrowing owls use an extremely resourceful, if slightly gross method to trap prey. One of the burrowing owl's favorite meals is dung beetles. And what do dung beetles love? That's right, animal feces. So, the burrowing owl will collect the feces of any animal it shares territory with and arrange it around its burrow. Then they simply wait for the beetles to arrive. While the beetles are busy eating the feces, the owls dive in for a beetle buffet.

Rollers are dung beetles that roll dung into a ball, then bury it for food storage. The ball may weigh ten times as much as the roller.

Many owls are nocturnal, but burrowing owls hunt day and night. Feeding six to eight chicks keeps them busy in the spring.

DID YOU KNOW?

Some scientists believe that decorating their burrows with mammal dung has the added benefit of disguising the burrowing owls' scent from predators.

AMAZONIAN ANTS

Allomerus decemarticulatus is a tiny species of ant found in the Amazon rain forest in Brazil and French Guiana. They live in one particular species of tree that they have a mutually beneficial, or symbiotic, relationship with. The ants keep the tree free from other insects that would eat it, and in return, the tree provides them with shelter and food. The shelter is found in leaf pockets, a space in the plant between the leaf and stem. The food is sweet nectar. Each tree is home to a colony of about 1,200 ants, with 40 or so in each individual pocket.

Once an insect lands, the nearest ants grab it and hold tight. They need strong jaws to do this. Then more ants arrive. They pull the prey flat and tear it apart.

TEAM TRAPPING

By working as a team, colonies of ants are able to trap prey several times bigger than an individual ant. They accomplish this by building a hollow platform from hairs they've cut from the tree. They then spread a fungus found in the ants' homes over these hairs to hold them together. After the platform is built, the ants then chew tiny holes into it, in which they hide with their wide-open jaws sticking out. When an insect like a grasshopper lands on the platform, it's seized by many pairs of jaws and pulled flat. Other ants then swarm and **dismember** the prey. The various parts of its body are then delivered to various parts of the colony.

DID YOU KNOW?

Of the over 12,500 classified species of ants, *Allomerus decemarticulatus* is the only one known to use traps.

To fool insects, the ants make their hollow traps look like they are part of the stem of the tree, but just a bit wider.

MESMERIZING STOATS

Stoats are half the size of a rabbit, but strong enough to grab one. They bite the neck and grasp the body with their short front legs.

Stoats are small, sleek mammals that are closely related to weasels and ferrets. They're found in mostly northern climates all over the world. They live in underground burrows that have already been made by rodents they prey on. Stoats are **carnivores** and survive on a diet of mostly rodents, with birds, fish, and even lizards eaten occasionally. One of the stoat's more challenging types of prey is rabbit. The problem is, rabbits are much faster than stoats. So, once the rabbit realizes it's being hunted, it makes a speedy retreat.

The fur of stoats turns mostly white in winter climates. This fur is also called ermine.

DANCES WITH DEATH

To prevent this, once a stoat locks eyes with a rabbit, it engages in one of the most **bizarre** mental traps in the animal kingdom: it dances.

Once a stoat has a rabbit's attention, it begins flipping and flailing on the ground. The rabbit becomes so entranced that it forgets all about running away, and while the stoat is dancing it is also slowly inching closer to the rabbit. Once it's finally in range, the stoat pounces, killing the rabbit with one bite to the back of the neck.

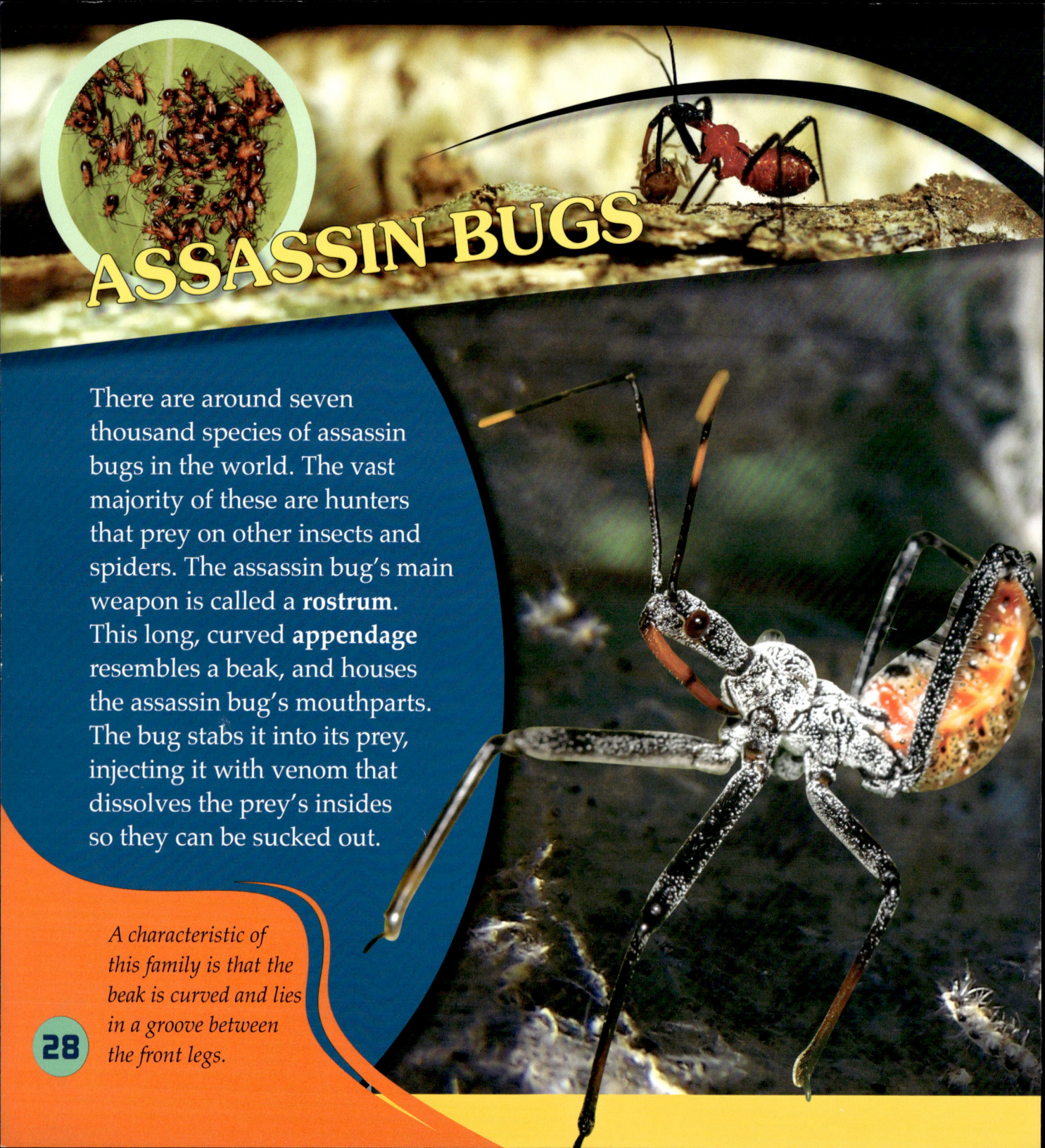

ASSASSIN BUGS

There are around seven thousand species of assassin bugs in the world. The vast majority of these are hunters that prey on other insects and spiders. The assassin bug's main weapon is called a **rostrum**. This long, curved **appendage** resembles a beak, and houses the assassin bug's mouthparts. The bug stabs it into its prey, injecting it with venom that dissolves the prey's insides so they can be sucked out.

A characteristic of this family is that the beak is curved and lies in a groove between the front legs.

TRAPPING THE TRAPPER

True to their names, assassin bugs are fearsome killers. They prey on species that are traditionally thought of as skilled hunters. One species, from Australia, has a diet that consists entirely of spiders. This in itself isn't unusual, but the way that it attracts its prey certainly is. The assassin bug uses the spider's own web to confuse and trap it. The assassin bug is able to pluck the threads of a web in a way that imitates the vibrations made by trapped prey. The spider, thinking it has caught a meal, rushes over, only to be made into a meal itself. This type of mental trap is known as aggressive mimicry.

Assassin bugs are strong. They can stab prey like this spider repeatedly with their beak while using powerful front legs to hold it down.

GLOSSARY

APPENDAGE A part that is attached to something larger and sticks out from it.

BIZARRE Very odd or strange.

BURROW An underground hole or tunnel dug by animals to live in.

CAMOUFLAGE Colors, textures, or materials that help animals blend into their environment and escape notice.

CARNIVORES Meat eaters.

DISMEMBER Break up or tear into pieces, especially used for a body.

EVOLVE Change over time.

HABITAT The environment that an animal lives in.

LARVA A stage of life before full adulthood for certain animals. For example, a caterpillar is the larval form of a butterfly. More than one larva are called larvae.

PREDATOR Any animal that hunts and feeds on other animals.

PREY Any animal that is hunted and eaten by other animals.

PROTRUDING Sticking out from something.

ROSTRUM Piercing mouthparts of assassin bugs.

SCAFFOLD A raised platform.

VENOM A poison made by some animals that either paralyzes or kills prey.

FOR MORE INFORMATION

Further Reading

Burnie, David. *Predator*.
New York, NY: DK Publishing, 2011.

Murawski, Darlyne. *Ultimate Bugopedia: The Most Complete Bug Reference Ever*.
Des Moines, IA: National Geographic Children's Books, 2013.

Seidensticker, John. *Predators*.
New York, NY: Simon & Schuster Books for Young Readers, 2008.

Tait, Noel. *Insects & Spiders*.
New York, NY: Simon & Schuster Books for Young Readers, 2008.

WEBSITES

For web resources related to the subject of this book, go to: **www.windmillbooks.com/weblinks** and select this book's title.

INDEX

A
alligator 20, 21
Amazon rain forest 24
ant(s) 5, 19, 24, 25
antlions 18, 19
apex 21
arachnids 7
assassin bugs 28, 29
Australia 16, 29

B
Brazil 24
burrow 14, 19, 22

C
camouflage 10, 13
carnivores 26

D
Darwin, Charles 10
Darwin's bark spider 10, 11
dismember 25
doodlebugs 19
dung beetles 22

E
ermine 27

F
French Guiana 24
funnel web 9

G
glowworms 16

H
habitats 9, 21
hunting 5, 12, 21

I
insects 7, 12, 13, 16, 21, 24, 25, 28

L
larvae 5, 16, 30

M
mental trap 4, 29
mimicry 29

N
New Zealand 16

O
ogre-faced spiders 12
orb web 8, 9, 13

P
predator(s) 4, 5, 17, 21

R
rostrum 28

S
silk 7, 8, 9, 10, 11, 13, 14, 15, 17
spinneret 7
spitting spider 15
stoats 26

T
tangle webs 8
trapdoor spider 14

U
United States 20, 21

V
venom 7, 11, 15, 18, 28